FOREIGN PLANES IN THE SERVICE OF THE LUFTWAFFE

FOREIGN PLANES IN THE SERVICE OF THE LUFTWAFFE (1938–1945)

Jean-Louis Roba

Pen & Sword
AVIATION

First published in Great Britain in 2009 by
Pen & Sword Aviation
an imprint of
Pen & Sword Books Ltd
47 Church Street
Barnsley
South Yorkshire
S70 2AS

ISBN 978-1-84884-081-2

A CIP catalogue record for this book is
available from the British Library

Typeset in Sabon 11/13pt by
Concept, Huddersfield

Printed by the MPG Books Group in the UK

Pen & Sword Books Ltd incorporates the Imprints of Pen & Sword
Aviation, Pen & Sword Maritime, Pen & Sword Military, Wharncliffe
Local History, Pen & Sword Select, Pen & Sword Military Classics,
Leo Cooper, Remember When, Seaforth Publishing and Frontline
Publishing.

For a complete list of Pen & Sword titles please contact
PEN & SWORD BOOKS LIMITED
47 Church Street, Barnsley, South Yorkshire, S70 2AS, England
E-mail: enquiries@pen-and-sword.co.uk
Website: www.pen-and-sword.co.uk

CONTENTS

PROLOGUE

From the end of the Second World War up to the present day, many authors have asserted the *'invincibility of the German Airforce'* as proof that the Third Reich had prepared for a war of aggression. This is a very simplistic vision, as the new German Luftwaffe was only created on 15 May 1933 (the first fighter unit being raised on 20 April 1934). Indeed, to raise such a force (forbidden by the Treaty of Versailles), the recently elected German government had to first assemble personnel ad hoc (initially ex-soldiers of the Great War coming from the Imperial Airforce as with Robert Ritter von Greim, from the Navy as with Theo Osterkamp, or from the Army as with Albert Kesselring) before launching a large programme of plane building. This was an arduous task to complete in five short years, but through competence and desire for revenge the Luftwaffe units appeared on time nearly every month.

In Spain, German specialists could examine captured Soviet planes (such as these Polikarpov I-15s lined up after the Nationalist victory). But as they were sent to the famed test centre at Rechlin, no Soviet planes could be included at that time in the Luftwaffe.

Another Soviet plane used by the Republican Airforce in Spain was the beautiful bomber Tupolev SB-2. One of them is seen here being examined by German personnel. SB-2s will later be used in numbers by the Luftwaffe.

Even if the involvement of the flying components of the Condor Legion in the civil war of Spain from 1936 helped the Luftwaffe to gain some experience in new tactics, this could in no way boost the production of planes limited by the capabilities of the aircraft industry.

Despite the reputation for German seriousness, the building of the Luftwaffe remained quite anarchic, and some important tasks had to be neglected due to lack of time or capabilities. Therefore, contrary to the simplifications of the above mentioned authors, the new (and too rapidly built) German Airforce was handicapped by many Achilles' heels:

- the engineers did not have enough time to conceive a long range bomber (such as the future American **B-17**);
- the production of transport planes was limited, and throughout the war the Luftwaffe suffered severely from a lack of air supplies;
- the German industries having to build important war materials (guns, tanks, etc), and as everything had to be made from scratch, not enough aircraft were produced. So, at the time of the Battle of Britain (August/September 1940), British industries produced more fighters than their German counterparts (a fact largely unmentioned by the supporters of 'The Few').

Thus, before and during wartime, leaders of the Luftwaffe had to face a real problem: how to find enough planes for training, transport, fighting or bombing. Buying foreign planes was impossible due to lack of money, the normal desire to support local production and the natural distaste all pilots had for an unknown aircraft.

This is why, on all occasions, the Luftwaffe tried to include in its ranks foreign planes that had fallen into German hands. The Luftwaffe was therefore the airforce to have used the most captured planes alongside its own aircraft. That is the subject of this book.

CHAPTER ONE

BEFORE THE WAR

The lack of planes was so serious that the Luftwaffe included aircraft of foreign origin in its ranks even before the Second World War. The first such machines were Italian ones employed by the Austrian Airforce. On 13 March 1938, Adolf Hitler announced the reattachment of his native Austria to Germany. This 'Anschluss' was approved by the majority of Austrians and, at the same time the Führer made his entry into Vienna, the Austrian Army was absorbed by the Wehrmacht. Austria, ruined by the mad destruction of the Austro-Hungarian monarchy after the Great War, had no opportunity to launch local plane production and most of its military planes came from Italy. Their Fiat fighters were not of good quality (the best one being the **Fiat CR.32**) and, after a short presence in fighter units (presumably in JG 76 – the future JG 54 – a *Geschwader* composed of some ex-Austrian military flyers), they were replaced by Bf 109s and transferred to air schools. This handful of Austrian planes were probably used until 1941 when lack of parts forced them to be grounded (scrapped).

On 14 March 1938, the Schwechat (Vienna) Fighter Group paid a visit to its German counterpart, JG 132, based at Döberitz (Berlin). As the Anschluss *occurred a day only before, the Fiat CR.32s of the unit were immediately seized and repainted in the Luftwaffe colours.*

German and ex-Austrian pilots in front of CR.32s. This photo was probably of JG 76.

Fiat CR.32 No. 169 with German markings: a thin fuselage black cross and the swastika on a white circle with red background on the tail.

This Fiat CR.20, too obsolete to be included in the Luftwaffe, is used as a gate guardian in a German Airforce barracks.

The same CR.20 photographed from the rear.

Many future flyers wanted to be photographed in front of the first plane they saw in their time as a recruit.

Although Austria did not help to reinforce the Wehrmacht a great deal, the capture of Czechoslovakia must have been considered an 'El Dorado' by the German military leaders. Indeed, this country produced not only very good tanks and guns (e.g. in the well-known Skoda fabric) but modern planes as well, mostly in the Avia industry. To equip the powerful Czechoslovakian Airforce, foreign planes were also produced under licence: the French Bloch 200 bomber and the Soviet Tupolev SB-2 (under designation Avia B-71). From the period beginning 30 September 1939 (Munich Agreement) and ending a few days after 15 March 1939 (Hitler's entry in Prague and dissolution of the Czechoslovak Republic), the Luftwaffe began to include in its ranks an appreciable number of French, Soviet and Czechoslovakian planes. The fate of these planes was very different:

- **Bloch 200**: already obsolete, though the twin engine will nevertheless have helped the Germans by being used as a hack machine (mainly for transport). A few will be sent to *Flugschulen* (flight schools) to train future bomber crews.

On a Czech airfield. Two Bloch 200s (locally built under licence) as they were found by German troops.

An ex-Czech Bloch 200 (coded ??+TC).

Bloch BH+BPs used in the Second World War.

These German officers were probably transported by the Bloch 200 in the background.

- **Avia B-71**: usually liked by its new crews, this more modern bomber was mainly assigned to *Luftdienst* units, tiny detachments attached to airfields. These planes were used as liaison planes or to tow drogues to train Flak gunners. Many of these valuable planes were also employed in school units.

The triangle on the nose of this Avia B-71 indicates that the twin engine was one used in a Luftdienstkommando.

Good view of the glazed nose of this Avia B-71, photographed on a German airfield in 1939.

German ground crews pose in front of an Avia B-71 used in a second line unit.

An Avia B-71 R(?)G+BQ warms its engines at Mannheim airfield. Notice the large swastika on the fin.

- **Avia B-534:** this pleasant one-seater fighter was admired and praised by the new owners. As it was captured in numbers (probably more than 300 B-534 fighters of all types – including Bk 534), they were largely used in the German Airforce, a training centre for this type

A mixed batch of Czechoslovak planes captured in 1938: Bloch, Letov and, in the middle, an Avia B-534 protected by a tarpaulin.

Strangely, this Avia B-534, which seems to have recently fallen into German hands (see the Ju 52 in background) has maintained its Czech fuselage code, H4 (of 4th Air Regiment), although a swastika is already painted on its fin.

of fighter having to be created at Herzogenaurach airfield for the dispatching of the planes. But the Lutftwaffe did not acquire all the fighters as some of them had to be given to the airforce of Germany's new ally: the independent Slovak state. As the B-534 was a modern plane, they tried to include it in frontline units.

Formation of Avia B-534s at Herzogenaurach. A dispatch centre for that type of machine was created here.

Herzogenaurach. An Avia B-534 is pushed by mechanics to its take-off position.

On September 1939, a *Staffel* (squadron) of II./Trägergruppe 186 received a few B-534s. A few of them were equipped with arrester-hooks and structurally strengthened for testing on the future aircraft carrier *Graf Zeppelin*. The experiment would last only a few weeks, until the captured planes were replaced by Bf 109s

This B-534 photographed at Cuxhaven was probably one of the planes temporarily assigned to II./Tr.Gr. 186. Notice the swastika painted partly on the fin.

Three views of the same machine: B-534 SE+CJ. These camouflage/markings were typical of the German flying schools.

Avia B-534 No. 174 wears a production number on the fin.

and pressed into school units. Another *Staffel*, 3./JG 70, was also temporarily equipped with Avias. The sole B-534s remaining in German frontline units were planes transferred into LLG 1 and LLG 2, the glider combat wings. The Czech machines were employed

The Avia B-534 wears the insignia of the FFS A/B 4 flying school: a funnel (the famed 'Trichter' of Nuremberg) on a diagonally strip red and white shield. The school was transferred from Nuremberg to Oppeln, on the soil of ex-Czechoslovakia.

The RC+FS with modified canopy.

(alongside many other planes such as Ju 87s, Hs 126s, etc) to tow DFS 230s. In 1940 a handful of planes were temporarily painted in Polish markings to play the role of PZL fighters in the Carl Ritter picture *Kampfgeschwader Lützow*.

This B-534 No. 6 may have been plane No. 228, later fifty per cent destroyed in an incident at Langendiebach while serving in Erg.Gr. (S) 1.

Refuelling of B-534s on a German airfield.

Many ex-Czechoslovak planes had to be given to Germany's new Slovak ally. Here B-534s of that Airforce in USSR in 1941.

To ferry captured Czech planes to Germany, all available pilots were required. Here, Walter Roell (a future ace of the Stuka wing) is seen before taking off with a Letov S-328. Notice the strange markings.

- **Letov S-328:** this versatile two-seater fighter/bomber was already obsolete in 1939. It was nevertheless a tough machine and, as it fell in numbers (probably more than 200) into German hands, they could not be simply destroyed. It was discovered after a few months

A line of captured Letov S-328s freshly repainted in German markings.

Some Letovs came in special aerial units, as seen here in a NSDAP school raised for party members wishing to be trained as pilots.

that the S-328 was a good plane well appreciated by the German pupils who trained on it. As with the B-534, some samples were given to the new Slovak Airforce. The majority of the captured planes remained near the ex-Czechoslovakian territory on the airfields of Pardubice, Gutenfeld, Pilzen, etc, where flying schools

Letov S-328 CD+DE of the Nuremberg/Oppeln school.

A good view of the 'Nüremberger Trichter' on the S-328. The size of the plane is worth noting.

were established. As with the Avia B-71, the S-328 was employed in some *Luftdienstkommandos* (No. 7, 13 and 17) as liaison planes or to tow drogues for the Flak gunners. S-328s also operated alongside the Avia B-534 in LLG 1, as it was able to tow DFS 230

A German S-328 in flight.

Crash of an S-328 on Mannheim airfield. Apparently, its pilot does not seem to have been traumatized by the experience.

gliders. A few may have been engaged in *Störstaffel*, those units operating by night to harass Soviet troops. However, whether they were engaged in this role remains uncertain.

As for many other Czech planes, the Germans, lacking suitable machines in the flying schools, assigned all that could be found to the

To partially counter the lack of training planes, obsolete Czech planes were transferred into German flying schools. This Praga E-39 was disliked by pupils for having no brakes.

Flugschulen, as with some Type Es. They were not appreciated, being too old. Other Czech planes could enter liaison units and, as with the ex-Austrian Fiat CR.32, were used until lack of parts forced their grounding.

For the German Luftwaffe, the captured Czechoslovak planes were crucial. Even if front units did not benefit from those planes, liaison and school units were largely reequipped with Letovs and Avias.

This Czech Praga E-241 flew at Bönninghardt flying school.

This Benes Mraz 51 coded GA+AB was based at Prostejow, an ex-Czech airfield.

Another Benes Mraz 51 used as a liaison plane.

CHAPTER TWO

THE FIRST DECEIVING CAMPAIGNS (1939–1940)

On 1 September 1939, the Wehrmacht invaded Poland. Two days later, Great Britain and France declared war on Germany, and that day became the first one of the Second World War.

Even though Poland fell in a few days, aerial plunder was very meagre. Many of the Polish planes facing the Germans were destroyed in the air or on the ground. Western Allies who believed that the Polish army could hold out against German forces were deterred by Poland's quick defeat. The rest of the Polish Airforce escaped to Romania where planes and crews were interned. This was a win for the Royal Romanian Airforce, equipped at that time mainly with Italian and Polish planes (PZL 11, 23, 24 and 37). All the planes which fell into German

German flyers examine a depleted PZL 23 'Karas' on a recently occupied Polish airfield. A rare sight, as many Polish planes were destroyed in the air or interred in Romania.

Winter 1939/1940. These PZL 37 'Los' (Elk), well guarded, were probably soon scrapped. Their destiny may have been grander, however, as some were sold to the Romanian Airforce, equipped as light bombers.

hands were then scrapped. It seems that spares for PZL planes were later sold to Germany's new Romanian ally.

During the Phoney War, a few French planes landed partially intact on German soil, mainly reconnaissance planes lost or damaged in aerial fighting. But these were rare, and the planes were only briefly examined by German specialists.

Norwegian Caproni Ca.310 No. 507, examined by German troops at Stavanger-Sola.

The same plane from the other side. These bombers will never serve in the Luftwaffe.

On 7 April 1940, Operation Weserübung began. To counter an Allied landing in Norway (intending to 'cut the road of Swedish steel' to Germany), the Wehrmacht invaded Denmark and Norway. The Scandinavian campaign was hard and there was a great deal of aerial fighting and bombing. Losses were high on both sides. Danish planes were mainly obsolete and were grounded for months, Denmark not being officially occupied. The majority of the planes of the Norwegian Airforce were destroyed, a handful escaping to Great Britain (as with three German-built He 115s). German troops nevertheless found a few aircraft such as Caproni Ca 310 bombers, Gladiator fighters, Tiger

Wreck of a Norwegian Tiger Moth.

In this dump near a Norwegian airfield, a German Bf 109 E and, in the background, another Norwegian Tiger Moth.

Moth bombers and old Hover MF-11 seaplanes. They were studied but destroyed later due to lack of parts. At Kjeller airfield (near Oslo), German soldiers captured all the newly-delivered **Curtiss Hawks,** the first North American machines to enter the Luftwaffe. Some were used in flying schools but would soon be more intensively employed.

Belgian Aéronautique Militaire *had a sole fighter Squadron equipped with modern planes.*

These Hurricanes were mainly destroyed on the ground, and this plane was probably lost at Schaffen airfield.

On 10 May 1940, Germany launched Fall Gelb, the invasion of the Western Countries. It was a huge success, four countries being overwhelmed while the BEF (British Expeditionary Force) had to quickly evacuate.

The Great-Duchy of Luxemburg had no Airforce while the few planes of the tiny Belgian *Aéronautique Militaire* were rapidly destroyed on the ground. Later, in the plunder of Belgium, the Luftwaffe only recovered some light and sport planes (as with **Tipsy** or **Stampe & Vertonghen**), which were mainly used for entertainment by a few pilots until they ran out of parts. Two Renard prototypes were also studied but never really entered the Luftwaffe.

Plunder in the Netherlands was better. German specialists gained control of Dutch aircraft industries (such as Fokker and Aviolanda). Many planes of the ex-*Luchtvaartafdeeling* classed as obsolete were destroyed. The fine seaplane **Fokker T.VIII** was seized in some numbers (a few of them escaped to Great Britain and flew in Coastal Command) and later sent to the Mediterranean (Aegean Sea) to operate in recce and convoy protection. **Fokker G-1** was an interesting machine but produced in too small numbers to be used seriously in the German Airforce. Thus, they were transferred to flying schools.

A captured Belgian SV-5. Some of them were used in the German Airforce. Following reports of Belgian resistance, two or three of these machines were present at St-Trond (St Truiden) airfield in 1943 to train the young night fighter pilots of II./NJG1.

The tiny Tipsy, built at Gosselies, was another Belgian sports plane. We know that two samples of the plane were used by a Group of JG 3 while occupying that airfield.

This Tipsy seems to have been included in JG 2. It certainly flew a few months with German marking before being grounded (and scrapped) due to a lack of spares.

Hermann Göring after the capitulation of the Netherlands (in the white tunic). An ex-Fokker pilot of the First World War, he visited Schiphol airport to see the captured Dutch planes of Luchtvaardafdeling. In fact, only a few Dutch aircraft would enter the Luftwaffe.

This Fokker D.XXI, the so-called 'Fighter of the poor countries', still wears the insignia 'met de drie muisjes' (three springing mice) painted on some planes of the Dutch 1 Ja V.A. (1st Fighter Squadron).

Fokker G-1 No. 356 in front of a KLM DC-3 (wearing the special markings of civilian planes of neutral countries). While the fighter will enter the Luftwaffe, DC-3 will be seized by Lufthansa, the civilian German air company. Since, to reinforce the weak transport units, DLH had to transfer nearly all its Ju 52s to the Luftwaffe, the company tried to fill the gaps by requisitioning all possible civilian transport planes from those captured in the war.

Ex-Dutch Fokker G-1 in German markings under the snow (probably in winter 1940/1941).

A Fokker G-1 photographed at Schleissheim by a trainee pilot surprised by that 'Dutch shape'. It is probably the aircraft tested on the airfield in August 1940. This type of plane never entered frontline units and finished its career in school units.

A Dutch Koolhoven FK-51 after capture. As with Koolhoven, equipping the Belgian Aéronautique Militaire *and captured at the same time, it will be scrapped.*

Another Fokker which was used by the Luftwaffe was the Fokker T-VIII, a very good seaplane.

Patrol over North Aegean. The Fokker T-VIII were mainly used in Seegruppe 125, based at Skaramanga in Northern Greece, until they ran out of spares.

Soldiers find some rest between the wings of a Dutch training plane destined for scrapping.

This Fokker T-V bomber has been repaired by two mechanics but will still have a sad end.

CHAPTER THREE
THE FRENCH MANNA (MAY/JUNE 1940)

After the fall of France, the Wehrmacht found a great deal of plunder. The defeated country had been split in two with a '*Zone Libre*' (Free Zone) under the Vichy Government in the south. Many French planes escaped there or reached North Africa (controlled by Vichy) before the capitulation. Nevertheless, German troops seized some aircraft industries and large numbers of intact French planes which never arrived on the front following the disorganization of the last days of the western campaign, or sabotage by French communist workers who, linked by the German-Soviet Pact of August 1939, disturbed the deliveries to the front line units.

The French *Armée de l'Air* had a lot of different planes, some modern, some totally obsolete.

- the beautiful bomber **LeO 45** was captured in small numbers (it was produced in Southern France and Germany could not seize its factory) and seems to have been transferred to school units where the machine was well appreciated.

Many LeO 451 bombers were destroyed in combat against the Luftwaffe in May/June 1940.

Some Potez will enter the Luftwaffe.

Three Po 63s ready to be transferred to a Flugschule.

CHAPTER THREE
THE FRENCH MANNA (MAY/JUNE 1940)

After the fall of France, the Wehrmacht found a great deal of plunder. The defeated country had been split in two with a '*Zone Libre*' (Free Zone) under the Vichy Government in the south. Many French planes escaped there or reached North Africa (controlled by Vichy) before the capitulation. Nevertheless, German troops seized some aircraft industries and large numbers of intact French planes which never arrived on the front following the disorganization of the last days of the western campaign, or sabotage by French communist workers who, linked by the German-Soviet Pact of August 1939, disturbed the deliveries to the front line units.

The French *Armée de l'Air* had a lot of different planes, some modern, some totally obsolete.

- the beautiful bomber **LeO 45** was captured in small numbers (it was produced in Southern France and Germany could not seize its factory) and seems to have been transferred to school units where the machine was well appreciated.

Many LeO 451 bombers were destroyed in combat against the Luftwaffe in May/June 1940.

This LeO was captured while being overhauled in its hangar.

This good French bomber will enter in some numbers into the Luftwaffe.

A LeO 45 used in a German flying school.

This Potez 63-11 was captured on a local airfield.

- the **Potez 63-11**, a good machine (mainly used in recce), was captured in large numbers. In fact, many were destroyed in the May/June fighting, but German troops found many more on Méaulte and Les Mureaux airfields. Around 100 of those planes entered flying schools or the *Luftdienstkommandos* attached to the airfields. Later, some were sold to the Romanian Airforce.

But many other Potez 63 will be found in airfields near factories such as here (probably at Méaulte).

Some Potez will enter the Luftwaffe.

Three Po 63s ready to be transferred to a Flugschule.

German troops recovered not only complete planes but also vital parts of damaged/destroyed aircraft.

This is why the engines of this Potez 63-11 No. 585 are dismantled.

The more modern French fighter, the D.520, was engaged very late in the western campaign, losing some numbers in the bitter combat.

- the sleek fighter **Dewoitine D.520** operated for a long time in the new German flying schools, mainly at the recent *Flugschule* of Villacoublay. It was well appreciated by its pilots, who liked the modern machine. It was nevertheless too under-armed to enter in the German front units.

Survivors that fell into German hands were transferred to flying schools. Here pupils pose on a D.520.

D.520 No. 78 at Villacoublay air school.

Examining the engine of a D.520 at Villacoublay in 1942.

Bloch fighters were sometimes found intact on captured airfields. This Bloch 152 of GC I/8 was force-landed by its Czech pilot near Douai on 18 May 1940.

The planes of the French Armée de l'Air *were partly under Vichy control. Here at Tours airfield, German and French officials inventory the aircraft.*

- the **Bloch fighters**, considered too heavy to enter the German Airforce, were used in *Flugschulen*, where they were not as popular as the D.520. In 1941, many were transferred to *Luftdienstkommandos* to tow drogues for the training of Flak crews.

A Bloch 152 is dismantled to be ferried to Germany. These fighters were attacked by the new owners for being too heavy.

Nevertheless some Bloch were assigned to German flying schools, including this Bloch 152 photographed at Neudorf, base of FFS A/B 116.

12th March 1941. Crash of Bloch 151 ex No. 372 in a wood near Neudorf.

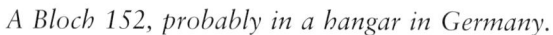

Its inexperienced young pilot had neglected to fill the tank of his machine.

A Bloch 152, probably in a hangar in Germany.

At Bourges, the Germans found many Curtiss H-75s ordered by the French Armée de l'Air from the USA.

- in Bourges (where they were assembled) and on the different airfields, the Luftwaffe captured many American **Curtiss H-75s,** in addition to those already discovered in Norway. Some were still in crates, having just been delivered to French harbours. The H-75 was a very good machine and German High Command ordered the transfer of around twelve of them to Döberitz (Berlin) to equip III./JG 77 (the ex-II./Tr.Gr. 186). As before (with the Avia attempt),

This plane still wears the insignia of the French GC (fighter group) I/4.

Curtiss H-75s were no newcomers, as some had already been captured in Norway a few months before.

the project was a failure, a few planes being damaged in the training. III./JG 77 quickly saw the US planes replaced by the 'good old Bf 109'. Three pilots of the units nevertheless flew H-75s painted with Polish markings to operate alongside 'Polish Avias' in Ritter's *Kampfgeschwader Lützow*. The Curtiss' were transferred to flying schools but soon most of them were sold to Finland, the new ally of Germany.

Facing the relatively large numbers of this modern American fighter, III./JG 77 was temporarily equipped with Curtiss H-75s This plane bears the notice 'Unklar' indicating that it is not fit to fly.

In September 1940, three pilots of III./JG 77 were required to play the role of the 'enemy' in the propaganda film Kampfgeschwader Lützow. A camera is installed in the nose of the H-75 manned by Leutnant Herbert Höhne.

False impacts were painted on the front of the canopy.

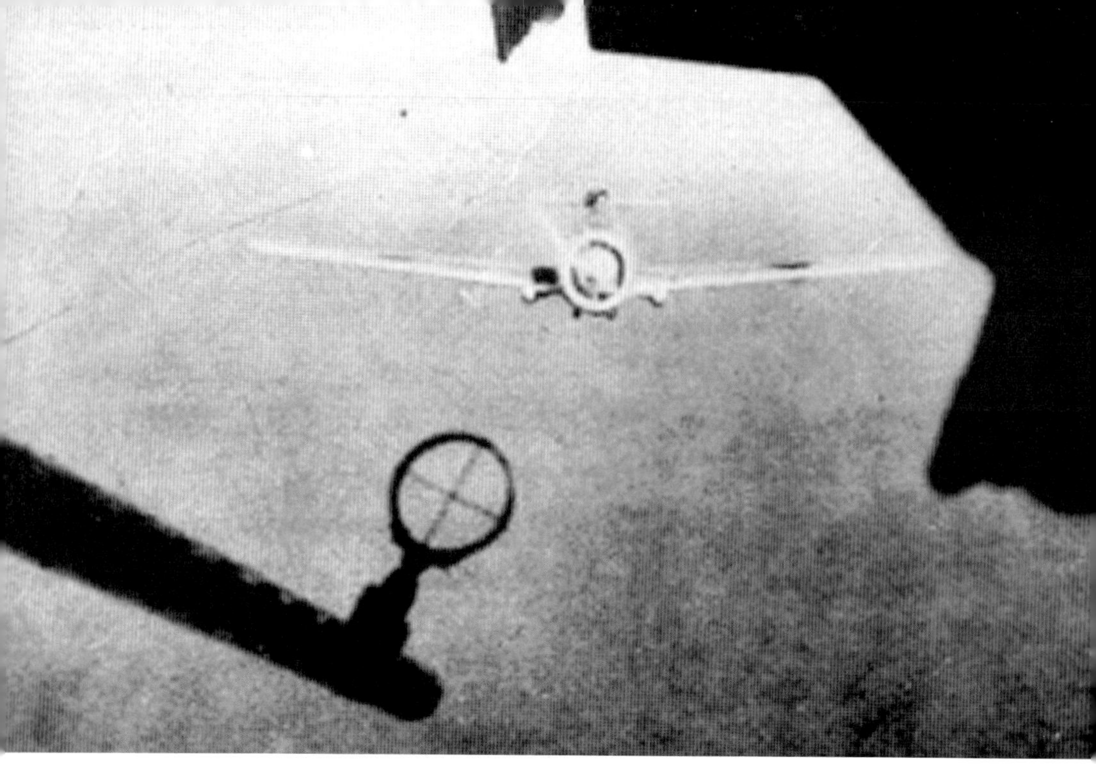

A still of the film 'Kampfgeschwader Lützow' showing the attack of an 'enemy' H-75.

Soon Curtiss H-75s were transferred to flying schools. Kurt Hammel (future fighter ace of JG 5 and JG 77) was one of the few pupils to be trained on this type of plane, the majority of which were later sold to Finland.

- a handful of **Morane-Saulnier 406s**, the second useful French fighter, entered the *Flugschulen*, but its value was too great to let it end its career in schools. At the end of 1940, ten MS 406s had been sold to the Finnish Airforce and others would follow. Later, after the dissolution of Yugoslavia, MS-406s were given/sold to the new Croatian Airforce.

These MS 406s, repainted with black crosses, have already received Stammkennzeichen *(factory codes) on the fuselage.*

A Morane Saulnier 406 found in a very bad state by the German troops on Maubeuge airfield.

A beautiful shot of a German MS 406. Possibly one of the planes sold to Finland.

A Caudron C-445 found at Issy-les-Moulineaux.

- the **Caudron C-445** was a very good multi purpose plane well appreciated by the French crews. It entered flying schools and some front units (such as *Jagdgeschwader*) as a hack machine. As the factory Caudron was at Issy-les-Moulineaux (near Paris) in the German occupied zone, the plane was produced by the new owners (at least 62 machines in 1941 and 334 in 1942). With the admiration of many German pupils, C-445 was one of the best French planes used in the Luftwaffe.

The yellow band painted around the fuselage of C-445 PO+CF was a typical mark of some flying schools.

Pupils and flying instructor in front of a C-445.

On the nose of this C-445 the insignia of FFS A/B 61 can be seen.

Photographed in May 1941 on Plantlüne airfield, this Caudron wears the insignia of FFS A/B 33, previously based at Seerappen.

A C-445 made a belly landing without too much damage, as the plane was sturdy. The insignia could be the one for Fluglehrerschule, *the school for flying instructors.*

Modern enough to be used in front units, some C-445 served as hack machines in some Jagdgeschwadern. *This one, photographed in North Africa, may have been attached to JG 27, or to a local command.*

At Escoublac, German troops found many training NAAs recently arrived in France.

- in the captures made in France, the Luftwaffe acquired another type of US plane. In February 1939 the French government had ordered around 400 NAA trainers (the *Armée de l'Air* didn't have enough pilots and so tried to accelerate the training of the pupils). Many NAAs were destroyed in May/June 1940 in incidents and bombing of airfields, but more than 150 planes were found intact (for example in Escoublac where the planes were mounted). The two types (NAA 57 and 64) were transferred to flying schools, being considered by its pilots as '*Amerikanisch*' (i.e. modern) with its large cockpit, a very good vision and a powerful engine. Trainer planes NAA 57 and 64 were, as with the C-445, well photographed on the airfields

Just captured, this NAA received a cross on the fuselage. Swastika and Stammkennzeichen *will later be painted on.*

An NAA in flight. This American plane was valued by future German pilots.

Having just received their pilot's insignia (pinned at the breast), young pilots want to take a photo in front of their beloved training machine. Note anti-reflection black paint in the front of the cockpit.

A bad landing in the snow (in German pilot's slang: a Fliegerdenkmal)*. This view gives an idea of the large size of the NAA.*

Formation flight of NAA in Toul airfield. This school often painted a large yellow band around the rear of the fuselage of its planes.

Grottkau flying school. The large canopy with its good visibility was appreciated by the young flyers.

- during the invasion, German forces also captured a lot of 'old' planes from the 1930s. Many were scrapped, but the lack of planes was so severe that some types were saved. So **MS 230** were for a time used in flying schools or second line units. Breguet 693 was tested by the Luftwaffe (following photos showing transfer to Germany) as were other types (e.g. Bloch 174). Many were

Some French planes of negligible value entered the Luftwaffe, including this Caudron Simoun liaison plane photographed at Bourges.

An obsolete Dewoitine D.510. It will probably soon be sent to the furnace.

quickly scrapped. The Caudron C-714 had showed its failures in the western campaign and was considered a very bad fighter. Six planes were nevertheless sold to Finland, but the other ones were scrapped (or placed as decoys on false airfields, the so-called *Scheinflugplätze*).

In the Western campaign, the Luftwaffe did not only capture French, Belgian or Dutch planes. Some RAF aircraft lost on the mainland were also seized: bombers which could not be blown up by their own troops, or fighters forced to land after a combat. We know that a few **Hurricanes** were captured intact; probably either one or three. The same went for **Blenheim** light bombers. The first complete **Spitfire** to

The MS 230 also entered second line units.

This obsolete MS 230 was given to a Hitler Jugend *unit to tow gliders.*

To find spares for the numerous captured French planes, dumps were visited, as with this one on the border of Cazaux airfield, south of Bordeaux.

French planes were not the only ones to be found or captured in France. RAF machines were also discovered. Here a destroyed Hurricane is examined by curious local youths and some Germans.

have fallen into German hands seems to be ZD-A of No. 222 Sq. whose pilot, F/O Falkus, was forced to land on Le Touquet airfield on 1 July 1940 after a fight with Messerschmitt Bf 109s and 110s. Tested and repainted, this plane will become the 'hero' of a famed propaganda film at the time of the Battle of Britain.

Wrecks were exposed in various exhibitions in Germany to emphasise the 'Great victory in the West'. This Hurricane, photographed at Leipzig, was definitely scrapped afterwards.

Some fighters were also found in an excellent state. This Hurricane of No. 97 Sq., in its box made of sandbags, seems not to have been blown up by mechanics.

A Hurricane in German markings photographed at the end of 1940. It is difficult to give the number of planes of this type which flew in the German Airforce.

This Blenheim of No. 114 Sq. was captured near Calais.

A Blenheim of No. 11 Sq. in use in the Luftwaffe.

Not all the wrecked planes found were scrapped. Some of these planes, lavishly repainted in German markings, were used as decoys on fake airfields (Scheinflugplätze). This Fairey Battle will end its career this way.

On 1 July 1940 after a dogfight, F/O Falkus of No. 222 Sq. was forced to land on Le Touquet airfield.

His ZD-A was probably the first Spitfire to have fallen intact into German hands.

Pilots of JG 26 were proud to be photographed in this – at the time – rare machine.

Tested and repainted, ZD-A will be used in a propaganda film, and this photo of a (fake) dogfight will be published in the renowned magazine Signal at the time of the Battle of Britain.

Arriving at Villacoublay airfield in June 1940, III./JG 26 find numerous French planes, including some prototypes such as the transport plane Air Wibault 100. As usual, the project will be studied by German engineers before being abandoned soon after.

CHAPTER FOUR

FACING GREAT BRITAIN (JULY 1940–JUNE 1941)

After France's capitulation at the end of June 1940, the Luftwaffe turned its attention to Britain. On some occasions, British planes damaged over the Channel had to land on the mainland. A few planes could then be captured in a relatively good state when their pilots made a belly landing.

On 15 August 1940, P/O Richard Hardy of No. 234 Sq. had his plane AZ-H (nicknamed 'Dirty Dick') damaged by Flak before being forced by a pilot of III./JG 53 to land at Cherbourg.

AZ-H (N3277) raised on its wheels, so that German pilots could photograph the wing machine gun emplacements.

Men of JG 53 were particularly interested in the personal insignia painted on the Spitfire.

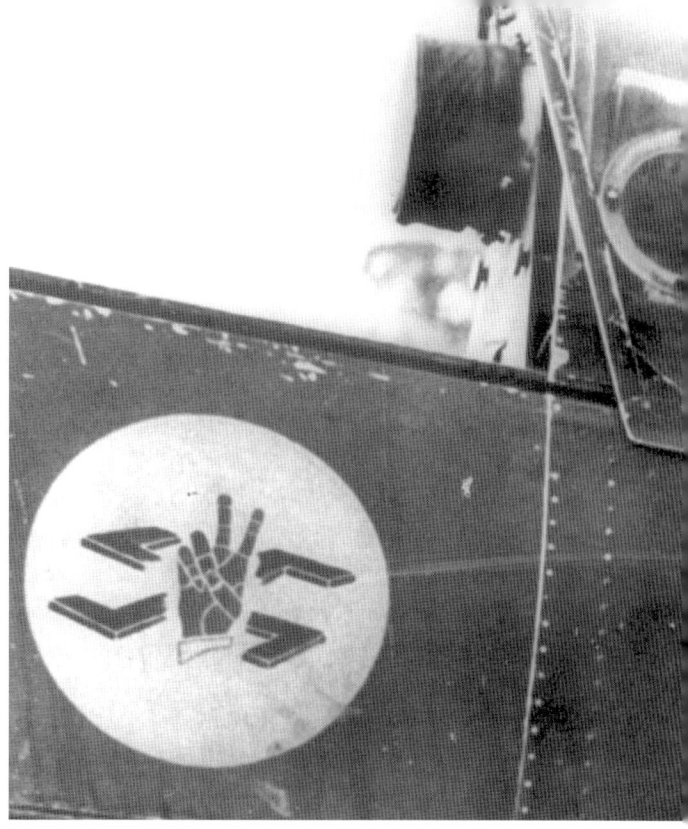

A better view of AZ-H's insignia.

Damage caused by the Flak shell are visible on the rear of the cockpit. Notice the first word of the nickname 'Dirty Dick'.

AZ-H is rapidly partly covered by camouflage. It will later be evacuated to Germany for testing.

A few bombers also made force landings and entered the German Airforce. Again, it is difficult to give numbers for those captures.

At the time of the Battle of Britain, Germany acquired new French planes. To reinforce its *Seenot* (sea rescue) units, the Luftwaffe bought a few **Breguet Bizerte** flying boats to operate alongside He 59s, Do 18s and soon Do 24s.

The same day (15 August), P/O Ralph Roberts of No. 64 Sq. landed his Spitfire SH-W (K9664) near Marck, the Calais airfield, after combat with 7./JG 26. This plane was also probably studied by the Luftwaffe, but its ultimate fate remains unknown.

On 16 and 17 August 1940, PRU lost two Spitfires engaged in a recce over the Ruhr. Both pilots became POWs. One of the planes seems to have been captured and was perhaps this plane, seen here in a demonstration in a German flying school in 1942.

To reinforce its Seenot *units engaged on the Channel, the Luftwaffe bought some French Breguet Bizerte seaplanes.*

This Bizerte may have been bought recently from the Vichy Airforce. It is seen alongside a LeO 451 already in German markings.

The German propaganda magazine 'Signal' published this photo of a Breguet Bizerte flying over the Channel.

On the night of the 26/27 August 1940, Hampden QR-P (P4324) ran out of fuel in an operation over Merseburg. The bomber made a perfect landing on the Vliehors sandbank of the Dutch island of Vlieland, its crew becoming POWs. QR-P was then test flown in Germany.

On 6 September 1940, engaged in a fight with JG 54, P/O Caister of No. 603 Sq. was forced to belly land near Guînes in the French Pas-de-Calais.

The fighter appears to be in good state, it was recovered by the men of the Jagdgeschwader.

Two opponents alongside: a Bf 109 of JG 54 and Spitfire XT-D (X4260).

Examination of the cockpit of XT-D.

XT-D under cover. This plane also seems to have been tested in Germany.

On the night 4/5 December 1940, Wellington LN-F (T2501) of No. 99 Sq. did not come back from a raid on Düsseldorf, becoming the sole loss of the mission. Disoriented, its crew landed on Vitry-en-Artois airfield where the plane was photographed by KG 53 soldiers based there.

When the Battle of Britain ended, the Luftwaffe launched the Blitz, the attacks by night on British cities. In response the RAF maintained its attacks over European mainland and the British planes once more fell into enemy hands. Many were tested at Rechlin, before being sent to various front line airfields to demonstrate the qualities and defects of the enemy planes.

LN-F seems to have been the first Wellington to have fallen intact into enemy hands. Repainted in German markings, it was transferred to Germany.

Wellington LN-F under the snow, probably on a German airfield.

We have no information about this Spitfire I of No. 74 Sq. which seems to have landed in very good condition on French soil.

This Hampden of No. 50 Sq. landed in Pfalz, probably returning from a bombing mission over Germany.

Some Hampdens were captured by the Germans in good condition but, until now, there was no proof that these bombers really entered the Luftwaffe.

This interesting photo published in the 'Der Adler' magazine probably shows a hangar at Rechlin where foreign planes were tested. In the background is a Wellington, apparently in very good condition. Abandoned aircraft were probably captured in May/June 1940, such as the French Breguet 693 or the RAF Fairey Battle of No. 150 Sq.

On 2 February 1941, No. 605 Sq. tried to intercept the pilots of I./LG 2 over the Channel. Sgt K.H. Jones was disoriented in the fight and landed his UP-M (Z2329) on the Belgian airfield of Koksijde (Coxyde). He was immediately captured.

Jones will later report that he fired a shot into the cockpit to destroy the machine. But despite this UP-M seems to be intact.

A captured Hurricane. Alas, we have no information about this plane.

On the night of 6/7 February 1941, the crew of a Wellington of No. 311 (Czech) Squadron landed on a French coastal airfield after an air attack on Boulogne-sur-Mer.

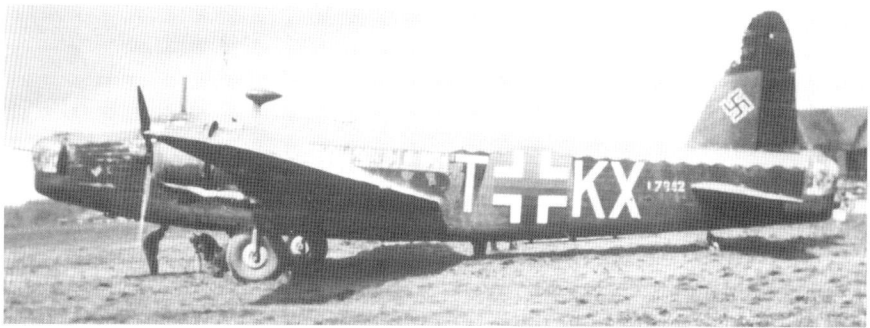

KT+X was repainted in German markings, and was perhaps the second Wellington to fall intact into German hands.

On the night of 17/18 February 1941, Whitley T4264 of Flight 419, a special unit dropping spies in occupied countries, was forced to land in a field at Waret-la-Chaussée near Namur (Belgium). The plane was apparently partly destroyed (by the crew?) and could only be used as source of spares (although we do not know of any flying Whitleys in the Luftwaffe).

If T4264 was useless to the Germans, they could at least recover the fuel, a rare substance at that period.

CHAPTER FIVE

MARITA/MERKUR AND BARBAROSSA (MAY–JUNE 1941)

On 6 April 1941, to repulse British troops from the Balkans, the Wehrmacht had to launch a new Blitzkrieg. Marita was an overwhelming success, forcing Yugoslavia and Greece to their knees. But not a single plane could be saved for the Luftwaffe. The Yugoslav Airforce lost its best planes (including Bf 109 Es) in the air fighting or on the ground, while other valuable aircraft (such as Do 17s) escaped to Egypt. The majority of the local aircraft found relatively intact were given to the new Croat Airforce, born from the ashes of the disbanded Yugoslav army. The Greek Airforce had some relatively modern French planes, but transport through the Balkan peninsula was too arduous, and all were probably scrapped.

A Yugoslav Blenheim destroyed by bombs.

Yugoslav Fizir FN burning. The fire was perhaps lit for the benefit of the Kriegsberichter (war correspondent) to make a striking picture. A proof of the low quality attributed by the Germans to the local planes found on the airfields.

Bücker 131 D WNr.482 was one of the German planes sold in 1939 to Yugoslavia. It was 'liberated' in Marita and ferried to the north with crude German markings (but still with the Yugoslav national cockade on the wings).

This plane will enter the Luftwaffe with Stammkennzeichen DA+RE.

A symbol of the German victory in the Balkans. On a Greek airfield (probably Larissa), a Ju 87 with the yellow markings of Marita has landed near the wreck of a blown up RAF Hurricane.

A Blenheim of No. 11 Sq. is dismantled in Greece. Its ultimate fate is unknown.

A Greek PZL 11 is examined by Landser *(German soldiers).*

In this dump, one can see Greek Bloch 152s and Po 63s. All these planes were definitely scrapped.

The same fate befell this beautiful but obsolete Potez XXV (with Hispano-Suiza engine).

On 22 June 1941 the great invasion of the USSR began. In their rapid advance, German troops overwhelmed many airfields dispersed all along the border, covered with planes of different values. The Soviet Airforce was at that time in the process of reorganization, and modern MiGs were found alongside obsolete biplane Polikarpovs. Even though

June 1941. A Bf 109 of JG 52 has landed on a Soviet airfield near a Jak fighter.

Many flyers wanted to be photographed in front of the modern Soviet aircraft.

Axis bombs destroyed a lot of those aircraft, hundreds of them were captured. However, only a few of them were used after testing in the Luftwaffe. Old planes were scrapped while modern ones were often sold to the Finnish Airforce. Indeed, accustomed to the cold of the polar

But a large number of obsolete planes will also be captured, such as these aligned Polikarpov I-15s.

Sometimes Soviet planes were delivered to the Luftwaffe. This Po-2 landed on a German-occupied airfield, its pilot probably being of Baltic origin.

winter, the Finnish Airforce specialists had mastered the wood/steel construction typical of a lot of Soviet planes.

These campaigns were thus deceiving for a Luftwaffe still desperate for new planes to fill the gaps in its erratic production.

The Soviet defector speaking with German high officers.

A Jak already in German markings photographed at Warsaw-Bilany, perhaps on the way to Germany.

A Tupolev SB-2 captured in relatively good condition.

The SB-2 will play the part of the hack machines initially performed by the Czech Avia B-71s.

Some of the captured Soviet planes will be used for special operations. On 6 July 1941, this Po-2 was found intact on Dünaburg airfield.

Two members of the Brandenburg unit (the so called 'Reichscommandos') examine the plane.

On 7 July two men wearing civilian clothes to pass as moujiks *board the plane.*

The Po-2 takes off to land in the Soviet lines with the two special agents.

A Lithuanian plane employed as a hack machine by the Luftwaffe on the southern part of the Eastern Front (Notice the Romanian liaison plane fleet in the background).

A variety of planes were captured on Soviet airfields. This training Jak may be used as a pleasure plane by some German flyers.

One of the few Polikarpov I-15s used in German flying schools.

A Polikarpov I-16 UTI (two-seater), probably in a Luftdienst *unit.*

A first type of the famed ground assault plane Ilyouchine Il-2 which probably force landed after a strafing. This sturdy machine seems to be only lightly damaged.

An Il-2 in the Luftwaffe. This plane is also of the first type (without the air gunner post).

German pilots assembled to be informed of and study the renowned Il-2.

A fighter Jak in German markings.

Another Jak used for a time in the Luftwaffe.

This MiG 3 must be the sample tested at Rechlin.

A MiG 3 serving in a Luftdienst *unit (as indicated by the triangle).*

CHAPTER SIX

ON ALL THEATRES OF WAR
(JUNE 1941–OCTOBER 1942)

Having noticed the transfer of nearly all German fighter units to the new Eastern Front, the RAF launched an ambitious aerial offensive over Northern France/Belgium, the so called 'Non-Stop Offensive'. It turned out to be very costly and a large number of British planes were destroyed, some of them falling nearly intact into German hands.

In the night offensives launched against German towns, British bombers damaged or disoriented landed in enemy-held territories and were captured. In this way, in August 1942, the Luftwaffe acquired its sole **Stirling**, a bomber already obsolete at the time.

In the theatre of the Mediterranean Sea, planes were only rarely captured by either side. The air fighting occurred mainly over the Libyan desert, and all planes which force-landed in the open were usually considered 100 per cent lost. Indeed, specialised recovery units

On 29 August 1941, in the execution of the famed 'Non-Stop Offensive', Spitfire PK-O (P8713) of No. 315 (Polish) Squadron was lost.

The fighter landed in Belgium on the strand of Westende and was quickly recovered by the Germans.

Fuselage of PK-O. This plane was probably sent to Germany, but we do not know if it was tested there or scrapped immediately.

A Wellington captured on a crude airfield in North Africa. As it was nearly impossible to evacuate these planes, souvenir hunters have already 'unclothed' it.

were scarce and didn't have enough vehicles to operate in the harsh desert conditions. The best way to save something was to dismantle the most valuable parts and leave the rest of the plane/wreck rusting in the sand.

A Lysander, probably found along the famed Via Balbia in Libya. The Luftwaffe acquired two such planes, probably captured when engaged in special missions in France. One of them was displayed in the static 'museum' of Nanterre.

A shot down Hurricane examined by German flyers in Libya.

The difficulties involved in ferrying planes are attested by this photo of a 'liberated' Hurricane at the end of 1941. In a counter-offensive, British troops found the captured Hurricane repainted in German markings. It could not be evacuated and was so retaken by the original owners.

This Blenheim was sent to Germany. It is possible that it was captured in the desert, as it was attached to an Australian squadron.

On the morning of 8 November 1941, pupils of EJG 26 stationed on Maldegem airfields were surprised to discover, facing their barracks, a British Wellington.

In the east, after the first success of Operation Barbarossa, Soviet planes were no longer captured on so great a scale. Some of the new machines were nevertheless tested by the German specialists.

This bomber, GR-Z (Z1277) of No. 300 (Polish) Sq. was disoriented in a mission over the Reich and landed intact in Belgium. On the same night, another Wellington from No. 304 Sq. landed on the Belgian airfield of St Truiden (St-Trond), and its crew were captured.

GR-Z was heavily photographed. Notice the insignia of the squadron.

After having been repainted in German markings, GR-Z departs for Germany.

On 12 April 1942, a Spitfire (AB131) of No. 521 Sq. engaged in a test flight landed by mistake on St Truiden (St-Trond) airfield, its Canadian pilot becoming a POW.

Personnel of II./NJG 1 based on that airfield took numerous photographs of the 'intruder', an ex-plane of No. 1401 Meteorological Flight.

Spitfire Vb RF-E (AA940) of No. 303 (Polish) Sq. was shot down in Circus 143 on 27 April 1942 and landed near Lille. The pilot became a POW. The fate of the plane is unknown.

Bergungskommandos *salvaged shot down planes all over Europe. This Spitfire, recovered on a beach in Northern France was probably heavily damaged by waves and salt water but could perhaps become a source of spare parts.*

All the wrecks were assembled in depots, as here in French St-Omer. Spare parts were recovered and the rest of the metal was sent to the furnaces.

The first giant Short Stirling bomber to be captured intact was MG-F (N3705) of No. 7 Sq. On the night of 15/16 August 1942, engaged in 'Gardening' (dropping of sea mines), with two engines and the compass out of action, it landed near Dutch Gorinchen.

The nose of the bomber was damaged. The plane had to be repaired before being repainted for its ferry flight.

On one of the large wings of the Stirling. This plane was studied in Rechlin before being used in April 1944 as a target to test new air-air munitions.

A Boston having made a belly landing, probably in France. It seems that no such plane was used in the Luftwaffe.

In the landing operations of Dieppe (19 August 1942), No. 350 (Belgian) Sq. lost P/O H. Marchal who was captured. His Spitfire Vb MN-Z (AR380), after recovery, seems to have been tested by the Luftwaffe.

At end of 1942, the transport units of the Luftwaffe were heavily engaged on the Eastern Front (Stalingrad) and the Med. Losses were high. To help quickly fill the gaps, Regia Aeronautica lent some Savoia Marchetti included in a special transport squadron, the Savoia Staffel. One of those planes is seen here on Maleme airfield (Crete).

Maleme. The Savoia Staffel is ready to fly to Africa. In fact the first Italian transport planes entered the Luftwaffe in April 1942.

Two German soldiers pose in front of a Savoia Staffel plane.

CHAPTER SEVEN

FRANCE AGAIN
(NOVEMBER 1942)

The Allied landing in North Africa (Operation Torch) on 10 November 1942 had an important consequence for France: the Wehrmacht went over the Demarcation Line between the two French zones to occupy Southern France.

Although some French flyers escaped by air with their planes to Morocco, Algeria or Tunisia, the greater part of *Aviation de l'Armistice* was overwhelmed on the captured airfields. Around 1,900 planes were so captured. This impressive number must be weighted by the fact that fifty per cent of these aircraft were old, no longer in use or in depots. Around 150 MS 230s had to be scrapped, as did 200 Caudron Lucioles. But this time Germany had taken control of some plane factories, such as Ossun (MS 406) and Ambérieu (LeO 451).

A Fw 190 (probably of JG 2) has landed on an airfield in Southern France, base of a Bloch 152 unit.

At Montpellier airfield, German officers talk with French Bloch pilots, probably to prepare for the occupation of the area.

German administrative officers verify the condition of French planes in the dump near Montpellier airfield.

*Around 1,900 French planes were captured in the ex-*Zone non occupée. *But, as one can see on this picture, many were only scraps.*

As the Italian Army took part in the invasion of Southern France, and as *Regia Aeronautica* suffered heavily in Northern Africa, the captured planes had to be divided after very hard negotiations between the two Axis partners.

Lioré and Olivier factory of Ambérieu were seized in November 1942.

LeO 451s could prove valuable to the Luftwaffe.

- the bomber **LeO 451** would soon interest the Luftwaffe, as German transport units were about to be decimated in the efforts to supply 6th Army at the Stalingrad and Tunisian bridgeheads. The LeO 451s were thus transformed into transport planes, becoming LeO 451 T (T for 'Transport'), many being included in the newly created IV./TG 4. It was not a real success, but the addition of the LeOs in the *Transportgeschwader* helped to lighten the pressure on the TG. Italy was able to borrow some of these bombers.

The Morane Saulnier factory of Ossun was also captured by the Germans.

MS 406s were too old to be used in the Luftwaffe. Only a handful of planes were assigned to Flugschulen, *while many planes were sold to Croatia or Finland.*

Some Potez 63-11 were also captured and transferred to flying schools.

A Po 63 in Flugschule *Pau.*

The good fighter Dewoitine 520 had to be shared with the Italians. The majority of those ex-fighters entered the Luftwaffe. Here are some D.520s on Toulouse-Blagnac.

- thirty of the old but still effective **Dewoitine 520s** entered the Italian Airforce. The rest rejoined the other D.520s already in *Flugschulen*. Around fifty of these machines were sold to the Bulgarian Airforce, mainly to replace their obsolete Avia B-534s. One year later, in October 1943, Bulgarian D.520s fought against US bombers over the Balkans.

Flying instructors in front of a D.520 at Orange.

A D.520 before its ferry flight to Bulgaria. Along with dozens of other Dewoitine fighters, it will reinforce the Bulgarian Airforce.

Fliegerdenkmal *of a pupil at Pau.*

D.520 taking off from Pau airfield.

D.520 over the Pau area.

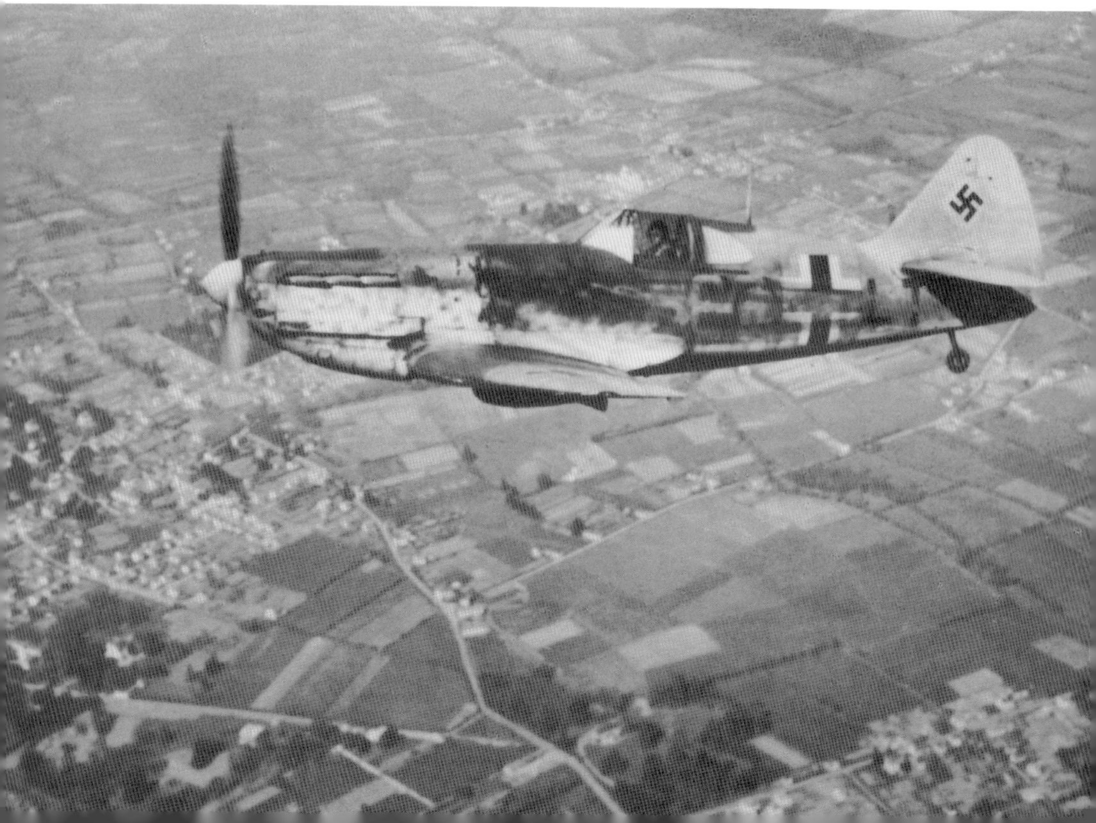

Bordeaux-Mérignac. A line of Bloch 174s. Many French planes served in second line units as liaisons or hack machines.

- some **Morane 406s** were found in depots. They were already too old to be useful for the German war effort. They were reactivated in Ossun, sent to a few *Flugschule* or sold to the Croat and Finnish allies.
- around 170 **Bloch fighters** (152 and 155) were captured. Many had to be overhauled. They were mainly transferred to *Flugschule* or to *Zielgeschwader* (the ex-*Luftdienst* units).

A Bloch 155 in the Fluglehrerschule. *This school, established at Orange, trained the candidate instructors.*

Flying instructors of Fluglehrerschule *Orange warming themselves in the Provence sun. In the background is a Bloch 155. Around twenty samples of this plane were captured in November 1942.*

- more than fifty of the valuable **NAA 57s** were captured, and reinforced the *Flugschulen* ...
- ... as did some Caudron **C-445s** still in use in the ex-*Armée de l'Armistice*.

Two mechanics posing on an NAA.

New NAAs were found in Southern France.

This good trainer will be appreciated in the flying schools.

A couple of NAAs in a Flugschule.

All the other valuable planes were posted to second line units, mainly as hack machines.

In 1943, German engineers tested Latécoère 299, whose prototype fell into their hands.

Latécoère 299 suffered an accident on Toulouse-Francazal airfield. One can see here the large size of the plane.

Laté 299 was repaired but never entered the Luftwaffe. This prototype will be destroyed in in its hangar in 1944 by Allied bombing.

CHAPTER EIGHT

'THE YANKS ARE COMING ...' (NOVEMBER 1942– SEPTEMBER 1943)

This period was catastrophic for the Wehrmacht, which suffered two severe setbacks in these months: the capitulation of the 6th Army at Stalingrad (January 1943) and the loss of Tunisia (May 1943).

In the air, the USAAF began to operate actively from its English bases. The first attack of B-17 bombers occurred on 17 August 1942 and, slowly, American planes intensified their actions. In this period, two

B-17s operated over France from 17 August 1942, and the first Flying Fortress to fall into German hands was captured on 12 December 1942.

B-17 41-24595 'Wulf Hound' of 303rd BG was forced to land on the Dutch airfield of Leuwaarden while engaged in a raid against Romilly.

four engine bombers (**B-17** and **B-24**) were captured. Nevertheless, it took months for the Luftwaffe to make them operational again. A RAF **Beaufighter** seems to have been captured, but we do not know where or when.

The B-17 was quickly repainted in German markings but its first flight in the Luftwaffe didn't happen until March 1943.

The original serial of the B-17 was maintained in spite of the repainting of 'Wulf Hound'.

The position of the left fuselage air gunner was heavily photographed.

'Wulf Hound' was visited by many German fighter pilots. Here, the Kommandeur of II./JG 26, Major Wilhelm-Ferdinand Galland discusses the bomber after having examined it. On 17 August 1943, he will be killed over Belgium, shot down by P-47s escorting Flying Fortresses.

The weak points of the Flying Fortress were underlined with white stripes. Here are the fuel tanks.

When the Danish Army was disbanded at the end of August/beginning of September 1943, the Luftwaffe recovered some planes (including at least twenty-one **Fokker D.XXIs**) in good state. It is doubtful that these obsolete machines spent long in the Luftwaffe, and the majority seem to have been scrapped.

While dogfights occurred over Europe, in North Africa Axis troops retreated into the Tunisian pocket. German troops could capture enemy planes, like this US Airacobra, but it is unlikely this plane could be ferried to the other side of the Med.

German soldiers pose on a shot down US Kittyhawk in Tunisia.

On 20 February 1943, B-24 D-1 41-23659 'Blonde Bomber' landed on the Sicilian airfield of Pachino.

Having been captured on Italian soil, the bomber naturally became the 'property' of Regia Aeronautica, being initially tested at Guidonia.

On 19 June 1943, 'Blonde Bomber' flew to Rechlin to be tested by the German specialists. Italian pilots were in exchange invited to try B-17 'Wulf Hound'. On its arrival the B-24 wears its US camouflage with Italian Savoia crosses. On 8 September 1943, when Italy broke its alliance, 'Blonde Bomber' remained in Germany, being repainted in German markings before presumably entering KG 200.

Spitfire AH-E (B5540) of No. 332 (Norwegian) Sq. was shot down in the Netherlands by JG 1. Its pilot, 2nd Lt Jorgen Nils Fuglesang, became a POW. The plane seems to be intact, but we do not know if it was salvaged by the Luftwaffe.

With such high losses of Allied planes on European soil, specialists were trained to study the new war material. Here, a Beutefeldwebel *examines an American bomber lost in Europe.*

Not all captured planes joined the Luftwaffe. This captured Spitfire was destroyed in a hangar on Bernay airfield (France) by allied bombs.

At the end of August 1943, the Danish Air Force was disbanded and its planes seized by the Germans. Around twenty Fokker D.XXIs were captured, but were probably all scrapped.

In this period, the Luftwaffe seems to have included an RAF Bristol Beaufighter in its ranks, but we do not know any more.

We do not know the origin of this Airspeed A.6 Envoy, photographed in a flying school. Perhaps a civilian plane found in the Baltic states.

CHAPTER NINE

ITALY: *IL RICCO BOTTINO* (SEPTEMBER 1943)

Οn 8 September 1943, Italy suddenly dropped out of the alliance. The German troops were not totally surprised, and some fights occurred between the troops of the ex-allies. The Italian army was disarmed in the areas controlled by the Wehrmacht and many planes were captured. On 7 November of the same year Generaloberst Alfred Jodl announced that 4,500 Italian planes were so seized. Today, historians believe that *Regia Aeronautica* only had 1,300 planes at that time, and only half of them were in a fit state to fly. Jodl's number certainly included all

After the Italian capitulation of 8 September 1943, German troops seized Regia Aeronautica *planes. Many were damaged, like these Savoia, probably photographed at Metato, the Pisa airfield.*

Men of the 'Überführungskommando General der Fliegerausbildung' on Gorizia airfield, waiting to ferry Caproni Ca. 313 or 314 to Germany. These planes wear a large white fuselage band denoting that they are captured aircraft to be ferried. Most of these men will soon be killed in a crash.

planes captured (e.g. civilian aircraft), in addition to the ex-French planes (D.520, LeO 451, etc) included in the Italian Airforce ten months before. Nevertheless, more than 1,000 planes were so acquired, and this *ricco bottino* (rich booty) had to be saved by the Germans.

A Caproni is refuelled before the flight.

A photo for the family.

First, specialists had to verify if the planes were able to fly to Germany. Then, to ferry those armadas, all available pilots were required. In Southern Italy, II./JG 77 temporarily had no planes. The pilots were then called to the north to ferry Fiat CR.42s and other machines to Munich. Transport pilots were called from their units to

Pordenone airfield. A German pilot crashed with an Italian fighter.

The burial of the unfortunate ferry pilot in a hangar of Pordenone.

do the same job. It was still not enough. The Luftwaffe then had to resort to creating short-lived units for transferring planes to safe airbases. '_Sonderkommando Gaul_' was assigned mainly to the transfer of seaplanes to Kiel. Around ten complete crews of flying school instructors were assembled in an '_Überführungskommando General der Fliegerausbildung_'. These men were parted between Gorizia (Görz)

In the night, a few Italian planes were destroyed by partisans on an unknown Italian airfield. The fiat G.50 and Fiat BR.20 in the foreground seem to be intact.

Gorizia. A line of Nardi FN.305s ready for the transfer. Two tiny Avia FL.3s (one with camouflage) are on the right.

and Pordenone to fly Italian planes to Berlin or Lechfeld. These missions were the source of many losses. In these flights, with totally unknown planes (Caproni, Savoia, Nardi, Saimann), crashes occurred. Allied airplanes, marauding in Northern Italy, could shoot down ex-Italian planes (such as 'He 115s', in fact Italian seaplanes). '*Überführungskommando General der Fliegerausbildung*' was nearly completely annihilated in an incident where the plane transporting most of the unit was shot down in Northern Italy. Only a few men survived.

Not all Italian planes were ferried to Germany. As II./JG 77 was still without planes in the north, the *Gruppe* was equipped with Macchi 205s

A Fiat CR.42 at Gorizia.

An SM.79, the 'Gobbo' (humpback), at Gorizia. This particular plane was used as a night bomber in the Regia Aeronautica.

(whose production line was situated in Northern Italy) in an attempt to fight using Italian fighters. Macchi 205s were unfortunately too light for the Germans, and fatal incidents occurred in the training. In the ensuing engagements with US bombers, only two kills were made. At the end of

II./JG 77 was briefly equipped with Macchi 205 fighters.

A Macchi of II./JG 77.

1943, the Macchi 205s – replaced by Bf 109s – were transferred to the ANR, the Airforce of the new RSI of Benito Mussolini. A few other Italian planes remained in the country to serve as hack machines. Some of them were included in special or second line units as Organisation Todt (OT) e.g. for liaison duties.

This plane was too light to be used in the Luftwaffe.

Some incidents occurred with the Italian fighters, and the Macchi 205 were supplanted by the Bf 109.

The Macchi were then given to the Italian units of the ANR (Aviazione Nationale Republicana).

A 'Gobbo' being overhauled.

The proud crew after the repair of their SM.79. This plane may have been used as a hack machine by JG 77.

A Fiat G.50 in German markings. No. 352 is very odd (perhaps the designation of its ex-unit: the 352a Squadriglia).

In Germany, the majority of ferried Italian planes were transferred into flying schools: **Fiat G.50** or **CR.42, Macchi 205** or **202** ... all were appreciated by the pupils. **SM.82** and **Cant 1007** entered transport units to help to fill the gaps of the *Transportgeschwader*. The beautiful **Piaggio 108** was used in a few situations. In December 1943,

The G.50 will be appreciated by future German pilots.

This Macchi 202 was assigned to the Fluglehrerschule *at Orange in French Provence.*

Transportstaffel 5 was raised to operate with thirteen of the four-engine planes. This squadron would later receive a few Savoia Marchettis before being combined with TG 4. A sole Piaggio had been lost in more than one year of activity.

This other Macchi 202 was a plane of JG 103, an advanced school unit.

An SM.82 which will soon enter a German transport unit.

This Cant seems to have been a hack machine attached to a flying school.

Fiat CR.42s will be used in large numbers in flying schools, such as here in Toul.

A CR.42 at Toul. Notice the large yellow band around the fuselage.

Boarding a CR.42 in a flying school.

A CR.42 of JG 107.

CR.42 and pupils of the same class.

A Cant seaplane, probably recovered in the Aegean.

These Red Cross seaplanes were useful in island areas.

An SM.82 in a Fallschirmjäger *(paratroopers) school. Probably* Fallschirmschule 1, *which received SM.82s and CA.148s.*

German parachutists boarding a Savoia. The transfer of these ex-Italian machines could free Ju 52 or He 111 for other more aggressive duties.

A Savoia of III./TG 1 photographed in a supply flight to the besieged Axis troops in the Crimea.

Another Savoia of a German transport unit somewhere in the Northern Mediterranean Sea.

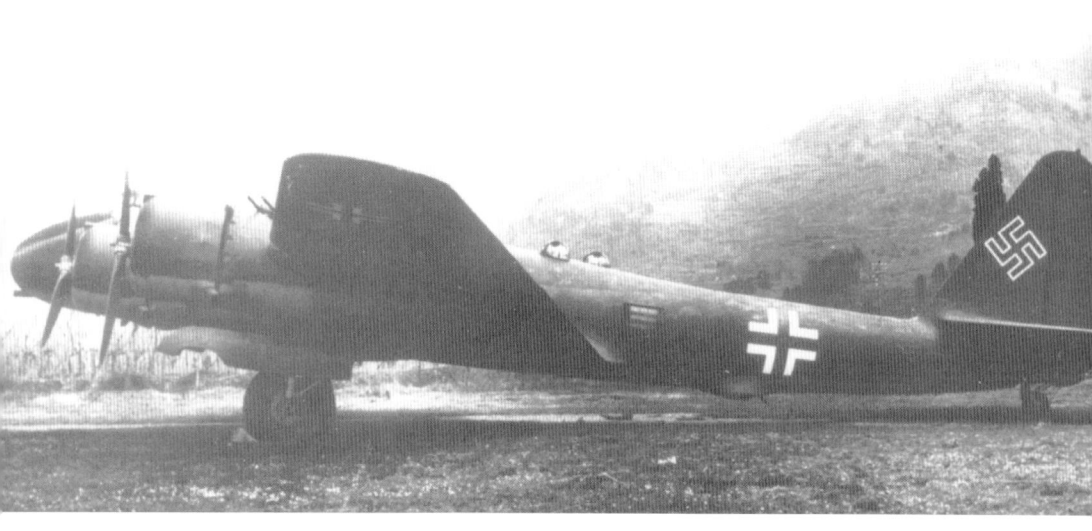

A Piaggio 108 (here the A version). This four-engine Italian plane was included in a special transport squadron, Transportfliegerstaffel 5.

CHAPTER TEN

UNTIL THE NORMANDY LANDING (OCTOBER 1943– JUNE 1944)

With the intensification of the air war over Europe, more and more USAAF planes were captured by the Germans. Some crashed in a very bad state, but these wrecks could still be studied. A handful of planes were captured intact and so could enter the German Air Force. Firstly, they paid visits to fighter bases to be presented to their opponents. Later, these planes were transferred to special units (such as KG 200) for missions behind enemy lines.

The sole B-26 of the Luftwaffe fell into German hands on 3 October 1943, when Marauder 41-17790 of 319th BG flying from Ireland to Scotland landed on the Dutch island of Noord Beveland (probably disoriented by signals from German radios). The bomber was presumably lost while being tested.

On 9 October 1943, B-17 F 42-30336 'Miss Nonalee II' landed at Vardö (Denmark), a victim of technical problems while engaged in a raid over Eastern Prussia.

'Miss Nonalee II' was intact and repainted as 7+8.

This bomber will be used to show the Flying Fortress to fighter pilots of units mainly operating in the east.

The ex-'Miss Nonalee II' was the victim of an accident. It is reported to have been destroyed at the end of the war.

On 14 October 1943, B-17 42-5714 of 91st BG is signalled 'presumed lost near Metz'. The bomber in fact landed at French Oron and was captured with its crew.

It was repainted DR+PE and tested by the Luftwaffe before joining KG 200.

161

The serial of the plane was repainted in little numbers on the fin.

A Mosquito landed on a French beach. Unfortunately, we do not have any more information about the plane.

A G.I. poses in the cockpit of a Fiat G.50. Probably found on an overwhelmed Italian airfield. The inscription states: 'Nur Überführungsklar' (only for ferry flights). The plane was therefore captured before its transfer to Germany.

A B-24, captured but unrecoverable.

The Schrott (scrap) depots will grow in Germany.

One of the most famous P-47s of the Luftwaffe, 'Beetle', landed on Carpiquet (Caen airfield) on 7 November 1943.

The fighter, a P-47 D 42-2240 of 355th FG, returning from a mission to Düren. It was initially repainted with the same codes (YF-U).

'Beetle' became T9+FK.

Flying from airfield to airfield, T9+FK will be closely examined by its opponents.

In this period, the Luftwaffe acquired at least one **B-26 Marauder**, one RAF **Mosquito**, two or three **Typhoons**, one **Lancaster bomber**, certainly some **P-47 Thunderbolts** and probably many other planes, such as **Spitfires** of the latter type.

In a P-47 cockpit (probably 'Beetle').

A good view of T9+FK with German fighter pilots.

In contrast, the numerous bombings and strafings targeting the airfields (mainly in the west) destroyed a lot of *Beuteflugzeugen* on the ground.

B-17 42-39759 of 571st BS/390th BG FC-G landed on 30 December 1943 in a field at Vimy in Northern France. The bomber was salvaged but was found nearly eight months later still stocked in a hangar of Buc, Versailles airfield.

Two Allied bombers in a hangar. We do not know if it was these two planes that were dismantled before their transfer to a static exhibition in one of the few Luftwaffe 'museums'.

On 4 March 1944, B-17 G 42-38017 XR-O was one of the three bombers of 100th BG lost in an attack on Berlin. Trying to land in neutral Sweden, the crew was in fact captured on Schleswig airfield. XR-O later entered KG 200.

Typhoon JR 319 of No. 175 RAF Sq. was lost on 16 March 1944 with another plane of its squadron in an attack on Villaroche, the Melun airfield. The machine is seen here recovering but we do not know if it entered the Luftwaffe. The German Airforce seems to have tested at least two Typhoons.

A Mustang wreck in a scrap depot waiting for its transfer to the furnaces.

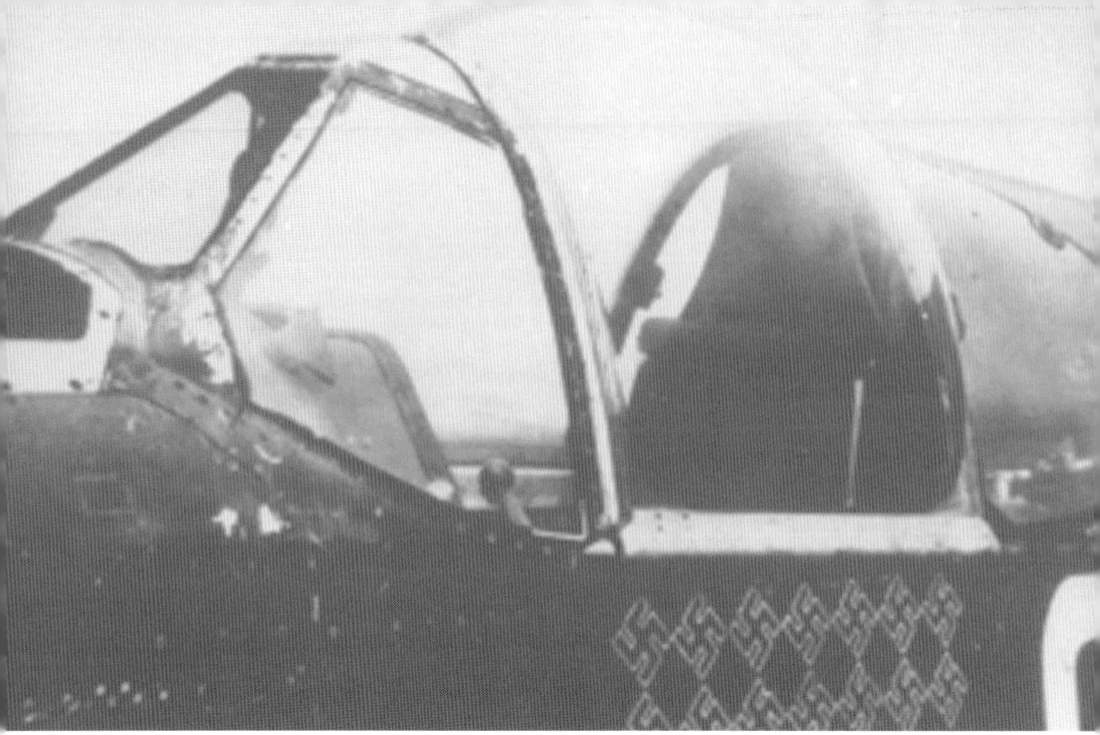

Another P-51 lying in the dump, which was apparently the plane of an ace pilot.

When escorting bombers to Germany, escort fighters could strafe enemy airfields, such as here near Verdun. An ex-French Caudron C-445 is the target of this attack.

On 20 March 1944, at least four P-47s were lost in bad weather and had to land on Belgian soil. This Thunderbolt of 356th FG/360th FS Sq. was captured at Neerwinden.

A P-47 dismantled in a German hangar, probably at St Truiden (St-Trond) airfield.

A B-24 that made a good landing is covered by nets to avoid any attack from the air.

The same for this B-17, which landed near a German airfield.

On 29 March 1944, B-24 H 42-52106 'Sunshine' of 449th BG/716th BS took off from Grottaglie to bomb Bolzano (Bozen). Probably damaged in a fight with the Bf 109s of II./JG 77, it landed on Venegono airfield.

The crew of 'Sunshine' surrendered and the Germans (mostly men of JG 53) could examine the four engines.

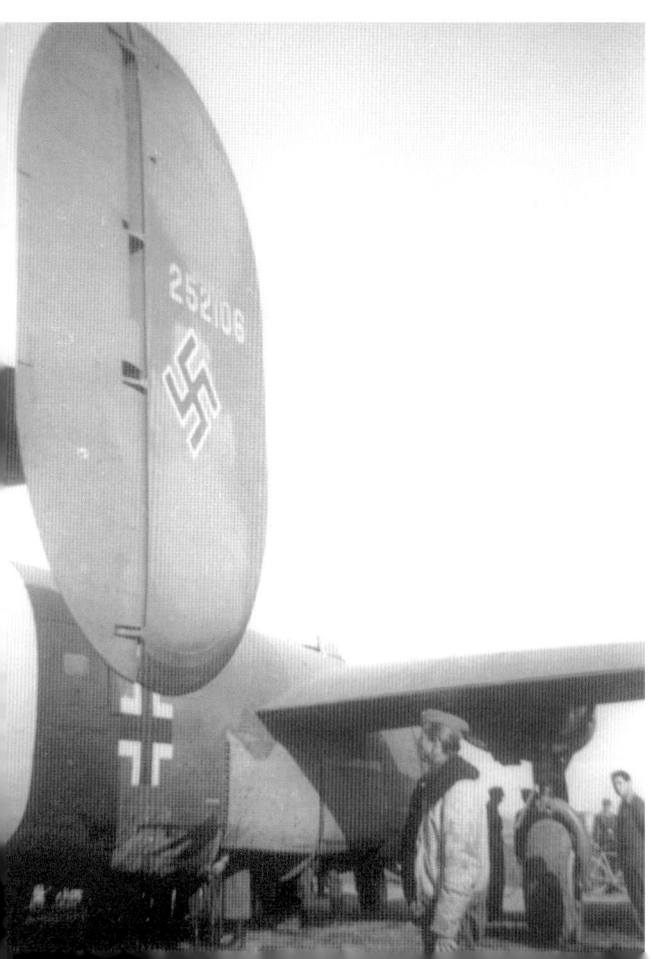

The nose armament of 'Sunshine' is heavily photographed.

A pilot of 1./JG 53, Fw. Harry Spröd, looks with some interest at the rear of the large bomber.

The following day, for the benefit of German propaganda, a rendition of the crew's capture was replayed with the 'real actors'.

A special crew came from Germany to ferry the repainted bomber to Werneuchen. 'Sunshine' will be used against the streams of RAF night bombers.

B-17 42-97218 JW-G 'Toonerville Trolley' made a very good belly landing at Bubach on 24 April 1944. It was definitely recovered by the Luftwaffe but we do not know if it was used or sent to the furnaces.

The Luftwaffe begins to suffer under the repeated attacks of USAAF. Here, on Pau airfield, some D.520s were damaged or destroyed.

P-47s strafing a LeO 451 on a French airfield.

The same LeO 451 after a second attack.

Romorantin airfield (near Paris) was also attacked and NAAs were destroyed.

What remains of an NAA at Romorantin.

On 13 May 1944, near Hanover, Spitfire PR.XI made a forced landing. It became T9+EK in the 'Zirkus Rosarius', the unit visiting the German airfields to show the enemy planes to the German pilots. Notice the very large swastika on yellow background.

The large black cross on the fuselage is also noticeable.

T9+EK could also be tested by some German experts, as here by Oblt. Günther Seeger of JG 53.

CHAPTER ELEVEN

THE END OF THE WAR
(JULY 1944–MAY 1945)

Progressing in France after having landed in Normandy on 6 June 1944, Allied soldiers discovered many wrecks of captured planes on ex-German airfields nearly intact. Some of those aircraft/wrecks were *Beuteflugzeuge* (captured aircraft).

To counter the second landing launched on the southern coast of France, German forces were dispatched to Provence, including II./JG 77, whose mechanics were transported by ex-Italian transport planes. But the Wehrmacht could not counter the enemy, and all France was being slowly liberated. On Belgian airfields, in September, other foreign planes of the Luftwaffe were also liberated.

Advancing in Normandy, US soldiers will find at Rannes the wreck of an obsolete French Bloch 210 in German markings.

We do not know if it was a hack machine or a decoy placed on a fake airfield.

In August 1944, II./JG 77 left Italy for Southern France. The ground crews were transported in Italian Savoias.

Flight from Ghedi to Orange.

In spite of the German retreat, air fighting was still intense, and new Allied aircraft fell into German hands. One of the most renowned was the **Mustang P-51** OP-K (44-14271) of USAAF 4th FG, one of the three planes of that type used by the German Airforce.

At Marseille-Marignane, US troops discovered ex-French LeO 451 bombers transformed into transport planes.

Inside a Marignane hangar.

On 13 October 1944, a few months before the end of the war, a pilot of the 15th Airforce 'borrowed' a recce **P-38 Lightning** to deliver it to a German-held airfield in North Italy. That man, a vehement anti-communist, wanted to help 'the fight against Bolshevism'. It was probably the third or fourth Lightning which entered the Luftwaffe, and this rare plane was certainly transferred to 'Zirkus Rosarius'.

At Chartres airfield, the wreck of a burned Potez 63-11 is examined by G.I.s.

Two captured B-17s destroyed in an allied bombing at Versailles-Buc.
42-30604 was a four-engine of 100th BG captured near Caen on 4 October
1942, while 42-39759 of 390th BG was lost at Vimy (Northern France) on
30 December 1943 (see photo before). These bombers may have been in too
bad a state to be evacuated to Germany and remained at Buc as sources of
spares for other captured Flying Fortresses.

Another B-17 wreck found at Buc.

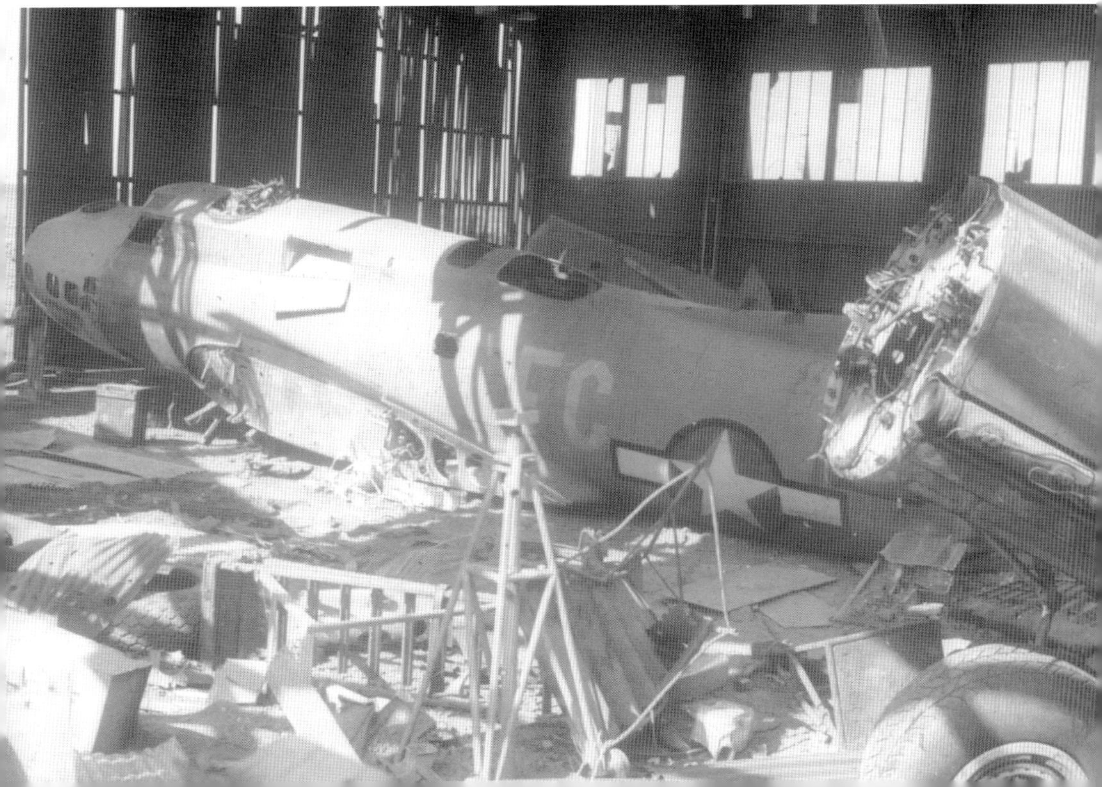

Still in Versailles, two wrecks 'liberated': a Typhoon (JP 845 of No. 485 Sq. lost near Abbeville on 21 December 1943) and a Mosquito.

In Lyon (probably Bron airfield), at least two wrecks of Reggiane 2002 were found.

These ex-Italian planes operated in Sonderkommando Bongart, *a special unit engaged against French partisans.*

On Melsbroek airfield (near Brussels), a Canadian soldier poses in a Dewoitine 520, an ex-French machine used by Zielgeschwader II. Before leaving the area, German mechanics removed the wheels of the plane.

Another D.520 destroyed at Melsbroek. Victim of a bombardment or blown up by retreating Germans?

A G.I. in front of a dump in Belgium or Northern France. On the top of the pile are the remains of an Re. 2002. Perhaps an abandoned plane of Sonderkommando Bongart which could not reach Germany.

On 12 September 1944, Cpt Thomas E. Joyce of 4th FG landed his P-51 D near Bernau which was quickly seized and repainted. This fighter will be one of the three Mustangs used by 2./Versuchsverband, based at Göttingen.

A good snap shot of the Mustang.

The P-51 with a German P-47 (probably 'Beetle').

The P-51 T9+HK with SpitfireT9+EK.

One of the few P-38s used by the Luftwaffe. The machine here was probably delivered by a defector in Northern Italy.

This P-38 was photographed at Luckau while being demonstrated to fighter pilots of JG 4.

In its advance west, the Red Army will capture some planes, such as this ex-Italian Savoia, used in a transport unit.

Another transport plane, an SM.82, captured by Soviet troops.

An interesting (but certainly not complete) list written at the end of the war gives an idea of some of the US aircraft captured from August 1944 to March 1945. Here are the intact (or nearly intact) planes which were likely prepared to enter the Luftwaffe:

- **B-17 F 230336**: captured at Bad Vöslau on 28 August 1944. Nearly transferred to KG 200 but lost before.

What remains of a German B-17.

Other Allied planes fell nearly intact into German hands. This P-51 of 354th FG/356th FS belly-landed in Germany on 1 December 1944.

- **P-51 D 413616:** captured at Oberhaching with only 20 per cent damages on 11 September 1944. Loaded on a train to Prenzlau on 10 January 1945.
- **P-51 4210358:** landed on its wheels at Ödenburg on 9 December 1944.

A Lockheed Lightning T9+MK in the winter.

B-24 KO+XA was initially a pathfinder plane captured on 20 June 1944 after being forced to land near Stettin. Transferred to KG 200, this four-engine plane was used in some special missions (deploying agents). Evacuated ahead of the Allied advance, the bomber eventually crashed when taking off from Quedlinburg.

The crew tried to save the plane. As it was impossible to repair KO+XA, it was destroyed by fire.

Near Herne (Germany), G.I.s seized a train loaded with some captured Allied fighters (P-47s and Spitfires). Consequently, these planes never entered a Versuchsverband to be tested.

- **P-51 41442:** captured with 10 per cent damages on 6 October 1944 at Reureld (*Note*: probably 44-144442 of 55th FG).
- **P-47 267324:** captured with 10 per cent damages at Gross-Sachsenheim on 2 February 1945.

P-38 T9+MK after its 'liberation'.

At Salzburg, the same fate befell B-24 '+KB' which fell into German hands on 4 February 1944 after a landing in France. This bomber was based in Austria for some supply flights from the Balkans to the besieged island of Rhodes.

The wreck of a German P-47 as found by G.I.s.

P-47 T9+LK 'liberated' in a better condition on Göttingen airfield.

- **P-51 D 4413905:** landed on its wheels at Barmersdorf on 20 February 1945 (a single propeller blade being bent).
- **P-51 D 411363:** landed on its wheels on 2 March 1945 at Zerbst.
- **B-24 441108:** landed on its wheels on 24 March 1945. Two engines damaged. Delivered to KG 200.

This Thunderbolt seems to have been a plane of 301st FS/332nd FG (the 'Tuskegee airmen'), captured on 29 May 1944 in Italy. Its pilot, disoriented, had landed on a German-held airfield.

This P-47 was probably partly destroyed by its last owners.

Three to five Thunderbolts were probably used by the special units of the Luftwaffe.

The remains of T9+RK, another Luftwaffe P-51.

Naturally, at that time, difficulties in communications largely hindered the transport of those planes and the majority of them could not be delivered as hoped to the German flying units.

Occupying a German airfield, men of the USAAF will discover some wrecks of American planes.

It is in their advances on German soil that Allied troops found the most numerous *Beuteflugzeugen*. Many were blown up by retreating mechanics, but nevertheless some ex-USAAF machines could be liberated.

Wreck of an SM.82 on a German airfield.

In May 1946, to commemorate the 'Great Patriotic War', German weapons were exhibited in a Moscow park. An SM.82 is seen in background.

At the same time, a Cant 1007 was part of an exhibition at Kiev.

CHAPTER 12

CONCLUSION

As stated at the beginning, the German Luftwaffe was the only air-force to have made so complete a use of its war plunder. Foreign planes used were mainly of Italian, French and Czech origins.

Until 1943, these aircraft were mainly transferred into flying schools, helping the German aircraft industries to concentrate on the production of fighters and bombers. But from 1943 the need for transport units was so acute that French and Italian machines were put to action in

A Caudron C.445 in German markings.

This other C.445 is painted in a beautiful blue colour. Note the black anti-reflect panel in front of the cockpit.

A Bloch 152 facing an Avia B-71. Notice the yellow colour covering the belly of the hack machine.

some special newly-raised units. We can see that on three occasions the Luftwaffe hoped to equip an offensive fighter unit with captured planes (Czech Avia B.534s in 1939, French Curtiss H-75s in 1940 and Italian Macchi 205s in 1943). All these attempts were totally unsuccessful.

A photograph of a LeO 451, most likely taken in the Med in 1943 or 1944. Here too, the ex-bomber has yellow paint on the lower structures.

Spitfire AZ-H a few hours after its capture on 15 August 1940. The damage caused by Flak is still visible. The fighter seems to be in the process of repainting.

German pilots examine AZ-H on a German airfield. Notice that the nickname 'Dirty Dick' was maintained.

A captured Hurricane used by JG 51.

Wellington LN-F after being captured on 5 December 1940 at Vitry-en-Artois.

LN-F in German markings.

German soldiers cut the red star from the fuselage of a captured Soviet plane. Proof that these planes were not very appreciated, and thus not protected by the Luftwaffe.

A Tupolev SB-2 (or an Avia B-71?) in a Luftdienst *unit.*

It is naturally difficult to give a number of the total *Beuteflugzeugen* used by the Luftwaffe, as eighty-five per cent of the archives of the airforce were lost, destroyed or burned in the war. We can only give an estimate: between 2,000 and 3,000:

- around 800/1,000 French planes;
- around 1,000/1,200 Italian planes;
- around 500/600 Czech planes.

A German Dragon Rapide. It seems that three of these planes were found in the Baltic States.

These few Dragons were used in the German Air Force until they ran out of parts.

A Kittyhawk found in the desert. These wrecks could rarely be salvaged, due to a lack of roads and transport vehicles.

The sole Stirling captured intact, MG-F (N3705) of No. 7 Sq, photographed on 16 August 1942 with a Bf 109.

An ex-Italian Savoir Marchetti 82 in flight.

As new documents/photos appear nearly every month, it is difficult to tell how many British/American planes were included in the Luftwaffe, being tested or used in special missions (e.g. in KG 200). We think that at least fifty USAAF planes were in service in the German Airforce

One of the P-38s used by the Luftwaffe.

Spitfire PR.XI T9+EK captured on 13 May 1944 near Hanover.

(fifty per cent were bombers). RAF planes perhaps numbered around forty. These numbers are those of the aircraft actually flown by German crews. Indeed, other captured enemy planes (such as a Lysander) were presented in static display in a few special 'museums' (like the French depot of Nanterre) to help the flyers to identify their enemies.

USAAF soldiers found this SM.82 on the edge of their newly occupied German airfield.

At Salzburg, a B-24 used to supply Rhodes island was liberated in May 1945.

APPENDIX
COLOUR PHOTOS OF THE
BEUTEFLUGZEUGEN

Photo Credit
Archive Gaston Botquin, Jean-Pierre Chantrain, Cynrik De Decker, Der Adler, Yves Empain, IWM, Sigrid Klessinger, Michel Ledet, Jean-Yves Lorant, Kees Mol, Eric Mombeek, Philippe Saintes, Signal, Hans-Heiri Stapfer, Peter Taghon, Axel Urbanke, USNA, Archive Jean-Charles Verrycken, Laurent Viton & Walter Waiss (Boelcke Archiv).

BIBLIOGRAPHY

Aubusson, Charles. 'Le convoyage des avions de prise italiens', *Avions*, No. 152 (2006).

Chapman, Richard. 'The Luftwaffe's Dragon rapides', *Aeroplane Monthly* (November 2007).

Cortet Pierre. 'Les biplaces d'entraînement North American', *Avions*, No. 58–64 (1998).

De Decker, Cynrik & Roba, Jean-Louis. 'RAF planes in the Luftwaffe', *Fly Past* {1992).

Joanne, Serge. 'Bloch MB-152', *Avions* (2003).

Neulen, Hans-Werner. 'Il ricco bottino', *Aero Fan*, special No. 2 (2000).

'Opération Etappenhase', Avions, No. 148 (2005).

'La Transportfliegerstaffel 5', *Avions*, No. 164 (2008).

Philpot, Bryan. *In enemy hands*, Patrick Stephens, 1981.

Roba, Jean-Louis. 'Les avions américains dans la Luftwaffe', *Avions*, No. 72 & 73 (1999).

Roba, Jean-Louis & Botquin, Gaston. 'Les avions français dans la Luftwaffe', *Avions*, No. 29, 30 & 31 (1995).

Stapfer, Hans-Heiri. 'Strangers in a strange land', *Squadron Signal* (1992).

Vrany, Jiri. *Avia B-534* (MBI 1994).

Vrany, Jin. *Letov S-328* (Jakab 2005).

INDEX